DANGEROUS WEATHER

WEATHER WATCHERS...

MARI SCHUH

ROurke
Educational Media

A Division of
Carson
Dellosa
Education

rourkeeducationalmedia.com

BEFORE AND DURING READING ACTIVITIES

Before Reading: *Building Background Knowledge and Vocabulary*

Building background knowledge can help children process new information and build upon what they already know. Before reading a book, it is important to tap into what children already know about the topic. This will help them develop their vocabulary and increase their reading comprehension.

Questions and Activities to Build Background Knowledge:

1. Look at the front cover of the book and read the title. What do you think this book will be about?
2. What do you already know about this topic?
3. Take a book walk and skim the pages. Look at the table of contents, photographs, captions, and bold words. Did these text features give you any information or predictions about what you will read in this book?

Vocabulary: *Vocabulary Is Key to Reading Comprehension*

Use the following directions to prompt a conversation about each word.
- Read the vocabulary words.
- What comes to mind when you see each word?
- What do you think each word means?

> **Vocabulary Words:**
> - *blizzard*
> - *drought*
> - *levees*
> - *shore*

During Reading: *Reading for Meaning and Understanding*

To achieve deep comprehension of a book, children are encouraged to use close reading strategies. During reading, it is important to have children stop and make connections. These connections result in deeper analysis and understanding of a book.

Close Reading a Text

During reading, have children stop and talk about the following:
- Any confusing parts
- Any unknown words
- Text to text, text to self, text to world connections
- The main idea in each chapter or heading

Encourage children to use context clues to determine the meaning of any unknown words. These strategies will help children learn to analyze the text more thoroughly as they read.

When you are finished reading this book, turn to the last page for an *After Reading Activity*.

TABLE OF CONTENTS

BAD WEATHER

What's that loud sound?

It's thunder!

A thunderstorm is on its way.

Thunderstorms are one type of dangerous weather.

People can get hurt.

We need to stay safe.

A room with no windows on the lowest floor of a building is a safe place.

A tornado spins across the land.

It moves about 28 miles (45 kilometers) an hour.

It's powerful!

9

Big waves crash on the **shore**.

It's a hurricane.

Hurricanes are tropical storms.

They bring wind and rain.

Sometimes, it is safest to leave the area when a hurricane is coming.

RAIN AND SNOW

Crops are dying.

The soil is very dry.

No rain has fallen.

A **drought** has begun.

The rain doesn't stop.

Rivers fill up.

The town might flood.

Levees help keep the water away.

A cold wind blows.

Lots of snow falls.

Roads are closed.

A **blizzard** is here!

STAYING SAFE

A loud siren blares.

A storm is coming!

We go to a safe place.

Listen to your local weather channel for safety tips during a storm.

7 DAY FORECAST
Weather Now

WED	THU	FRI	SAT
Heavy Rain	Heavy Rain	Scattered Storms	Scattered Storms
71	78	81	8
	63	70	

Scattered Storms

73

PHOTO GLOSSARY

 **blizzard** (BLIZ-urd): A big snowstorm.

 **drought** (drout): A long time when no rain or very little rain falls.

 **levees** (LEV-eez): Areas built up near rivers to stop flooding.

 **shore** (shor): The land along the edge of a river, lake, or ocean.

ACTIVITY: Tornado in a Bottle

Tornadoes are one type of dangerous weather. Watch a tornado form by making a small one in a bottle!

Supplies
two 2-liter (0.5-gallon) bottles
water
food coloring
glitter
duct tape

Directions
1. Fill one bottle about two-thirds full of water.
2. Add food coloring and a small amount of glitter.
3. Tape the two bottles together at their openings with duct tape.
4. Flip the connected bottles over so the bottle with water drains into the other bottle. Then, swirl the bottles by moving them in a circle.
5. Water will rush into the bottom bottle. A tornado will form in the top bottle!

ABOUT THE AUTHOR

Mari Schuh is the author of more than 300 nonfiction books for beginning readers, including many books about sports, animals, and stormy weather. She lives in Iowa with her husband and one very feisty house rabbit. You can learn more at her website: www.marischuh.com.

INDEX

AFTER READING ACTIVITY

Watch a weather report on TV. What kinds of weather might happen this week? How can you be ready?

Library of Congress PCN Data

Dangerous Weather / Mari Schuh
(Weather Watchers)
ISBN 978-1-73162-844-2 (hard cover)(alk. paper)
ISBN 978-1-73162-839-8 (soft cover)
ISBN 978-1-73162-851-0 (e-Book)
ISBN 978-1-73163-331-6 (ePub)
Library of Congress Control Number: 2019945030

Rourke Educational Media
Printed in the United States of America,
North Mankato, Minnesota

www.rourkeeducationalmedia.com

Edited by: Hailey Scragg
Cover and interior design by: Kathy Walsh
Photo Credits: Cover, Pg 1 ©Pobytov, solarseven; Pg 2-23 ©Pobytov, Pg 5 ©Romolo Tavani. Pg 7 ©edstrom; Pg 9 ©Minerva Studio; Pg 11, 22 ©tuaindeed; Pg 13, 22 ©David Sucsy; Pg 15, 22 ©tacojim; Pg 17, 22 ©eddtoro; Pg 19 ©Dakota Hillhouse; Pg 21 ©SpiffyJ